TWO CATS
and the
WOMAN THEY OWN

TWO CATS
and the
WOMAN THEY OWN
or Lessons I Learned from My Cats

PATTI DAVIS

illustrations by **WARD SCHUMAKER**

CHRONICLE BOOKS
SAN FRANCISCO

Thank you to Jay Schaefer, Micaela Heekin, Sara Schneider, and everyone at Chronicle Books who worked so lovingly on this project. Thanks also to Vicky Wilson for suggesting Chronicle would be the book's best possible home. Thank you to Ward Schumaker for his playful and sensitive illustrations. And to Aretha and Skeeter for their inspiration and continual life lessons.

Library of Congress Cataloging-in-Publication data available.

ISBN 0-8118-5166-4

Manufactured in China

Book and cover design by Joanne Lee

Distributed in Canada by Raincoast Books
9050 Shaughnessy Street
Vancouver, British Columbia V6P 6E5

10 9 8 7 6 5 4 3 2 1

Chronicle Books LLC
85 Second Street
San Francisco, California 94105
www.chroniclebooks.com

DEDICATION

*To my brother Ron, who has patiently
shared his wisdom and experience in the
mysteries and challenges of cat parenting.*

the ADOPTION

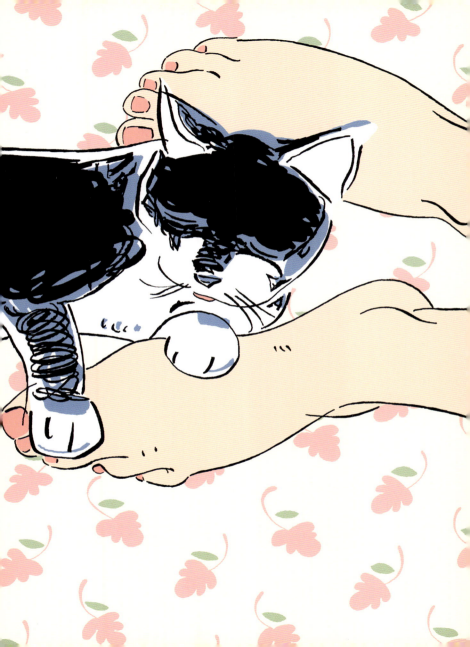

HER NAME IS ARETHA. She is small—only nine pounds—with a tail that never grew to proper cat length. (I've heard this can happen in utero when the developing kitten sits on its tail.) She is always formally dressed—a white and black "tuxedo cat." Four years ago when I lived at the beach, she belonged to my neighbor. Alas, she was from a broken home. When my neighbor's girlfriend moved out and left him with Aretha, his busy schedule didn't allow for a sufficient amount of cat time. So Aretha did what many of her species do: she picked up her little cat suitcases and moved—to me. She quite emphatically adopted me—trailing me everywhere, curling up in my lap whenever I sat down, meowing into the phone during even the most critical business conversations, and making very clear her choice of sleeping arrangements. It takes some adjustment to sleep with a cat wedged between your legs, but since I admired her self-confidence and air of authority, I wasn't about to argue.

I explained to her that I really knew nothing about living with a cat. I was far more familiar with dogs and would probably tend to treat her like a dog. She seemed OK with that, even walking downstairs with me at night to do her business outside in the sand, patiently assuming that I would soon get her a proper litter box. I did, of course, as well as an impressive collection of cat toys and the finest food I could find at the pet store.

After the death of my dog Sadie, who was my companion for ten years, I came up with various excuses not to get another right away: I was living in an apartment, I might be moving again soon, et cetera. I didn't admit they were excuses, but once Aretha adopted me, I realized I had been avoiding love. Sadie's death was so hard on me. I had been holding myself back from loving another animal in that all-consuming unconditional way most pet owners do. I didn't want my heart to break again. Once the cat door was put in, the litter box and food dishes were placed where Aretha seemed to want them placed, once she was officially mine—and I hers—I knew I had crossed an emotional boundary line.

LIFE LESSON

1

It's true that love can lead to sorrow and hurt, but avoiding love is never a good solution. Hearts are meant to be open and full, not kept safe behind walls. Pascal said, "When one does not love too much, one does not love enough."

the MOTHER'S DAY GIFT

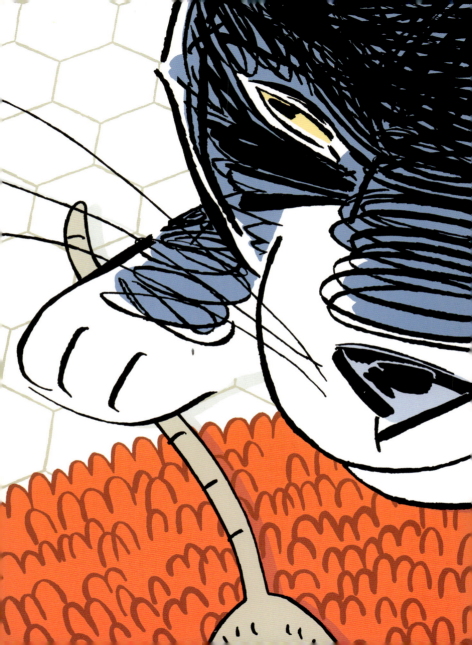

ARETHA AND I quickly developed a routine. She would come in at night, and I'd close the cat door; then in the morning, I would open it so she could go in and out at her leisure. We were still a new family when Mother's Day rolled around. Since it was Sunday, I stumbled out of bed at dawn just to open the cat door for her and then went back to bed. When I got up an hour later and walked into the bathroom, there was a large dead rat on the floor and a very proud cat sitting beside it.

"The good news is it means she likes you," my brother told me. (As a longtime cat owner he has been the recipient of many such gifts.)

I didn't want to hurt her feelings by removing the offending carcass, but of course I had to. As well as the bathroom rug. I did notice that Aretha looked a bit miffed. After all, she had gone to some trouble to find just the right Mother's Day gift.

LIFE LESSON

2

There is an art to properly receiving
gifts. Even if you don't like the gift,
you should cherish the giver and praise
her generosity.

a SAD TURN of EVENTS

ARETHA WAS INVOLVED in a rather amorous, and apparently monogamous, relationship with the cat who lived in the downstairs apartment. Spider was a handsome gray cat who often behaved like a dog. He would happily go on car trips with his parents, sitting up in the backseat or climbing into the front. Aretha forgave his quirks, and even before she adopted me, she would begin her days by going to my neighbors' door and waiting for someone to open it so she could go in and fetch Spider.

As men are prone to do, Spider began straying. We could never figure out where he went, but he was leaving more often and for longer periods of time. Occasionally he stayed away overnight. One morning, after being gone all night, he returned with a grunion in his mouth and offered it to Aretha. I'm sure she tried to convince herself that her boyfriend had spent the whole night grunion hunting.

The day came when Spider didn't return at all. We papered the town with flyers and called vets' offices and animal shelters, but after a week we had to admit that Spider was probably gone forever.

Aretha's grief was heart wrenching. She would wait at Spider's door, and when it opened, she would search for him inside, meowing mournfully. She carried toys around in her mouth, offering them to any human who knew Spider—as if the toys were ransom payments and could secure his return. She slept curled around my neck and almost never purred anymore. There was nothing I could do but comfort her—and hope that time and perhaps a new companion would ease her sadness.

3

You can't rush grief. It has its own timetable.
All you can do is make sure there are
lots of soft places around—beds, pillows,
arms, laps.

the NEXT ADOPTION

I FIRST SAW HER as a paw—a small gray paw sticking out from beneath a layer of newspaper, the same color as Spider, although tinier. I'd gone to the animal shelter to adopt a companion for Aretha—a kitten, so Aretha could retain her position as resident diva—and preferably a female, because I didn't want her to be jilted again by a wandering man. There were two other kittens at the shelter that day, playful and funny, eagerly looking out through the bars of their cages. Several people had already signed up, hoping to adopt them. No one had signed up for the three-month-old charcoal gray kitten hiding under newspaper. She had two days left before the shelter would euthanize her. I adopted her, though I couldn't take her home right away; the shelter required that she first be taken to a vet to be fixed.

At the end of the day, I came home with Aretha's new sister—her belly shaved, her tiny meows broadcasting her fear. I expected a bit more civility from my feline child. Certainly a dog would have been curious, nurturing, excited by this new addition to the household. But things are different in the world of cats. Aretha not only hissed at the frightened little kitten, she hissed at me, too. For days. It was high drama, and my brother's counseling that cats tend to be drama queens but do eventually relent wasn't making me feel better. The only consolation was that anger had replaced grief in Aretha's busy little head.

I named the kitten Skeeter because skeeting away from everyone and everything was what she did best—and constantly. At first, though, she managed to accomplish this skeeting feat without ever straightening her legs.

"Do you think there's something wrong with her legs?" I asked my neighbor as we watched this small gray kitten scurry across the floor with her odd low-to-the-ground gait. She moved like a frog—a very fast frog.

"No," he said. "I think she's just scared. She's somewhat feral—like she was never held or cuddled." The drama did end, as my brother predicted. One day I walked into the bedroom and found Aretha grooming Skeeter with her tongue, giving her new sister a luxurious bath. Soon they were sleeping curled around each other—and I had two cats wedged against me at night. They now wait for each other at the end of the day, neither one willing to come in alone, even when their canned food has been opened and the intoxicating smell is luring them. They prefer to dine together.

LIFE LESSON

4

You never go wrong when you choose
compassion over practicality. Choosing a
different kitten might have been more
logical, but my heart cracked open at the
sight of a little gray paw.

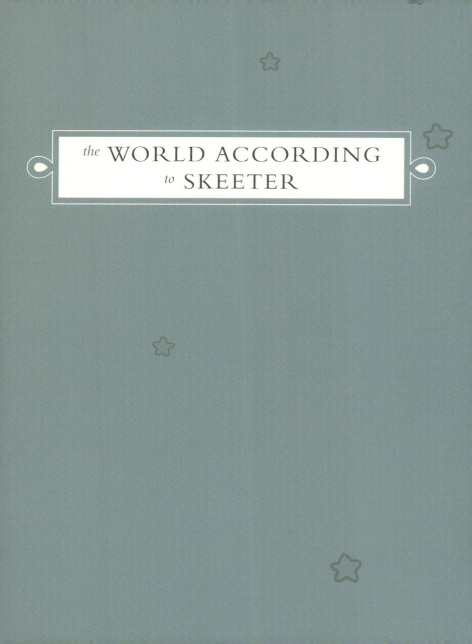

the WORLD ACCORDING *to* SKEETER

SOMEWHERE ALONG THE WAY, when she was an orphan living on the streets, Skeeter developed an extreme case of vigilance in regard to human beings. This is particularly evident in the daylight hours. She scurries across the floor like a cockroach, and if any visitor to my home dares to approach her, she will move faster than you would think possible, given that she is a bit hefty around the middle.

She has, however, figured out that night—the very late hours of night—is a safe time in which to ask for affection and cuddling. Three thirty in the morning is her favorite time. If I'm sleeping too soundly, pacing across my stomach is her chosen method of waking me. She then insists, with high-pitched meows, that I turn onto my side so we can properly "spoon." Once the desired position is accomplished and she is safely tucked into the crook of my arm, she commences that quintessential feline habit of kneading her paws (I call it making muffins). This can go on for quite a while, her meows now replaced by contented purring. But if I dare to move my other arm, she will leap up and off the bed, apparently remembering that humans—even her own human—can never be trusted completely.

Eye contact is also quite alarming to her. Together, we have developed a method that seems to work for her—most of the time. It's called "one hand, no eyes." If I want to comb her, put flea medicine on her, or even just stroke her during the dreaded daylight hours, I must approach slowly with only one arm extended (two arms might mean I am planning to grab her). And I cannot under any circumstances look at her. It's taken me a while to perfect this technique, especially navigating the approach without looking where I'm going.

Bringing Skeeter in at night is also tricky. Aretha bounds through the back door, eager for her canned food. Skeeter lingers on the back stairs, waiting for me to turn away, go into the kitchen, stand with my back to the door, and prepare their food while she slinks in. Only when she is sitting beside her dish can I move to the door, close it, and shut the cat door—all without ever making eye contact.

LIFE LESSON

5

Be understanding of what others have
gone through in their lives, even if it has left
them with some odd habits. There is no
such thing as normal—we're all a little quirky.

the MOUSE that GOT AWAY

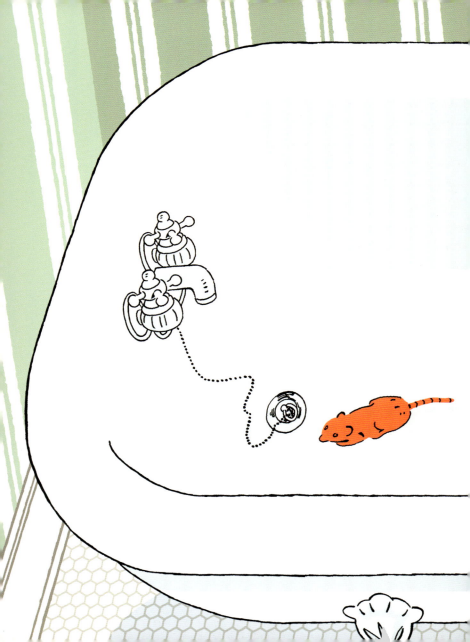

LATE ONE NIGHT, I was awakened by a loud crashing sound coming from the bathroom. I jumped out of bed, nearly colliding with Aretha, who was racing out of the bathroom, clearly frightened by the noise. In the tub, surrounded by broken pieces of a terra-cotta candleholder, was an equally frightened mouse. Luckily for me, mice are tiny and cute, and don't lunge to bite you if you pick them up by the tail (note: don't try this maneuver with a rat). I gently lifted the mouse up and carried him down to the beach in the dark, freeing him to find his way into someone else's home.

After her scare, Aretha had joined Skeeter under the bed, so she was unaware of my rescue efforts on behalf of the mouse. She assumed the small rodent was still on the premises. For the next couple of weeks Aretha slept in the bathroom, often in the tub, waiting patiently for the mouse to return. I tried petting her and cajoling her; I tried telling her in soothing tones that the mouse was gone, that he wouldn't be returning to the bathtub. But cats are genetically programmed for patience and tenacity. Tiny tigers, they can wait forever. Night after night, she staked out the bathtub, refusing to come into the bedroom.

Finally, after weeks of this, I was dozing off when I heard Aretha meowing on the floor right beneath me. When I sat up and looked at her, she scampered toward the door, then back to me, then back to the door again, obviously wanting me to follow her. I obeyed, wondering if her dreams had come true and the mouse really had come back. Not exactly. There in the center of the bathroom floor was one of her toy mice, which she had carried in and placed carefully. She looked at me, then at the mouse, meowing insistently as if she were really at her wit's end. "Do you get it now?" I'm sure she was thinking. "Humans are so dense sometimes. I hope I've finally made myself clear." I didn't know what to do, so I put the toy mouse in the tub, although I'm not really sure what that communicated to her.

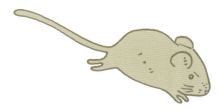

6

While it is important to face reality,
it's also important to dream. When we love
someone, we should gently urge her to
accept disappointments while never extin-
guishing her fondest dreams.

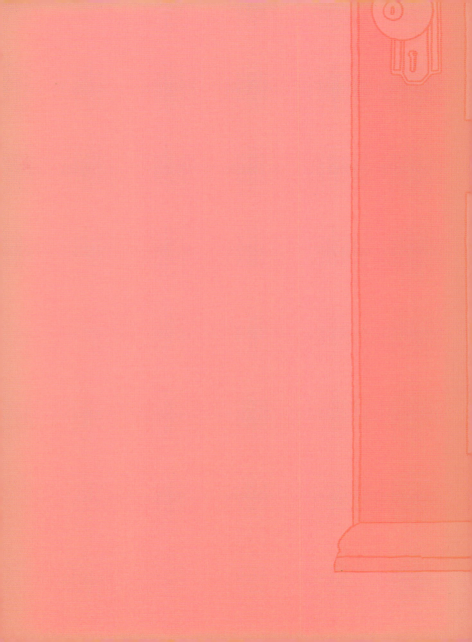

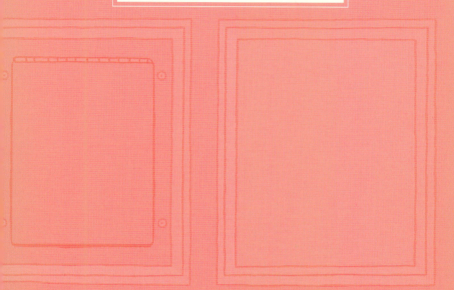

the BOYFRIEND

HE STARTED HOWLING outside our window at night. Then Skeeter brought him home with her and made it pretty clear that she was smitten. Lucas, a long-haired tuxedo cat, lived a few houses away from us at the beach and soon began visiting every day. There were evenings when I had to carry him home because he refused to leave on his own. Some mornings—I soon discovered—Skeeter would go to his house and fetch him. Aretha ignored him for the most part, although there was one day when I returned to find all three of them on the bed.

Some evenings, he was so desperate to see Skeeter that he would sit outside scratching and pounding his body against the closed cat door. I was forced a couple of times to call his father and ask him to please come collect this persistent Romeo. One night he hurled his body against the closed cat door and actually managed to push it in, thereby gaining access to his lover's home. He stood proudly in the living room, basking in the glory of his successful, although clumsy, way of breaking and entering.

I didn't mind him visiting, but Lucas had an unfortunate habit of spraying inside my apartment. I couldn't really blame him; his irresponsible owner had never had him neutered. But Skeeter's romance became a very smelly affair. I think I should buy stock in Nature's Miracle—God knows I've used enough of it.

LIFE LESSON

7

We can't choose our family members'
friends. Sometimes we don't understand
those relationships, but tolerance
is important.

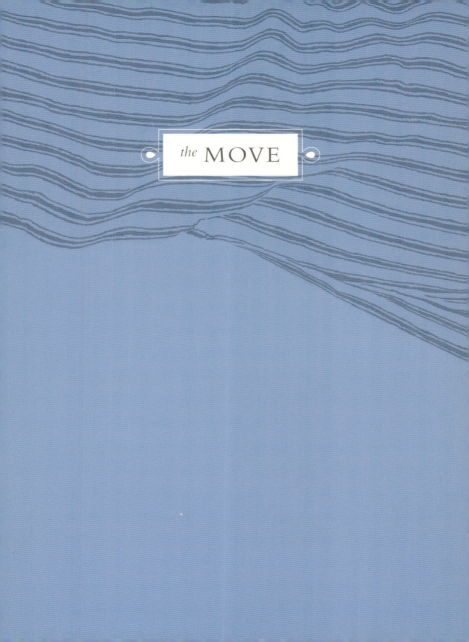

the MOVE

MOVING IS WAY UP there on the stress scale; I think it's right below divorce and a death in the family. Moving with cats comes with an added challenge: mental strategy. Specifically, how to conceal evidence of the impending move until that one fateful moment when you snag those clever felines, load them into their cat carriers and into your car, and then head on down the road to a new life.

Miraculously, I succeeded with no mishaps. I was haunted by warnings that, unless cats are kept inside for at least two weeks, they will leave and go in search of their former home. I had nightmares of Aretha and Skeeter traveling brutal miles, crossing highways, sniffing the air for whispers of the sea.

I didn't have to worry. They stayed under the bed for most of those first two weeks, emerging at times to sit at the windows and peer out at our new territory: a garden and trees—no ocean but lots of green. And we have more room inside—more closets to hide in, more corners to settle into when the late afternoon sun slants through, more rooms to hold more scratching posts and scattered toys.

There was one mishap, however. We now had a fireplace—a new thing for Aretha and Skeeter. One morning, while they were still under house arrest, I couldn't find Aretha. Moments before panic would have disabled me, she emerged from the fireplace. The white part of her was ash gray; actually, everything on her was ash gray. She had slipped around the chain-mail curtains and started up the chimney. Fortunately, Aretha likes baths, but even washing her didn't really get the sooty residue off. She was a smudgy little Cinderella, with no fairy godmother in sight. It took a week before her white socks were white again. What did happen faster was my solution for her chimney traveling: I ran out and got a solid screen to block the passage, which made for a very grumpy Cinderella—just when she was starting to have some fun.

8

Change is always hard, but time softens the rough edges and eases the pull of the past. Eventually, we all climb out from under the bed, and even the most unfamiliar places begin to feel like home.

SKEETER'S *in* LOVE, AGAIN

LATE ONE NIGHT, when a cat howling outside woke me from a sound sleep, my first thought was, "Oh no—Lucas followed us all the way from the beach." Skeeter bolted off the bed and ran eagerly to the window, probably hoping that was the case. Aretha opened one grumpy eye, undoubtedly thinking, "No, not again."

It wasn't Lucas. It was a short-haired gray and white cat with a skinny body and big ears. He was still there in the morning, having spent all night waiting for my girls to emerge from the house. Skeeter, of course, willingly approached him. Aretha hissed, flicked her tail at him, and went back inside.

He was a sporadic visitor—a stray, I quickly deduced, when I spotted him many blocks away and looking awfully ragged. He made one bold attempt to follow Skeeter in through the cat door. Bad move. Aretha sprang toward him and chased him down the stairs and up a tree. He was more tentative after that, waiting under a tree for Skeeter to come out by herself.

I haven't seen him in a while. I welcome the peace and quiet, but I don't like to think that he met some unfortunate end. Maybe courting Skeeter became too dangerous, with Aretha acting like Annie Oakley.

LIFE LESSON

9

Some of us have a more active love life than
others. Don't resent a friend's flirtations
just because you haven't had a date in a while.

the WORLD ACCORDING *to* ARETHA

EVERYONE TENDS TO have certain rules to live by. Aretha is no exception, and her rule is easy to discern: a place for everything and everything in its place. She carefully rearranges her toys on a daily basis, carrying them into one room or the other. If I dare to move one of them, I'm faced with a disgruntled cat sitting in the location she had chosen for said toy, giving me a stern, narrow-eyed look. Nothing will do except placing the toy back in that exact location. The closet door in the bedroom must stay partially open at all times because she often places toys in there amongst my shoes. I'm sure she has her reasons—I have no idea what they are—but when I inadvertently closed the closet door one day, she came to find me and meowed loudly until I figured out what I had done wrong and remedied the situation.

She also has strong ideas about appropriate behavior. It is apparently completely inappropriate for me to do any kind of physical exercise, like sit-ups or stretches, at home. If I insist on carrying out my desired exercise, I must do sit-ups with Aretha standing on my stomach, staring at me with a displeased expression. If I try stretching, she will run back and forth across my legs and occasionally swat at my toes.

Headstands are something I've had to give up entirely. Try standing on your head with a cat pacing back and forth in front of your face, meowing at you. It becomes very stressful.

I have seen Aretha clean up bits of food Skeeter has left on the floor, and I'm sure she is saying to herself, "If she would just eat a little slower, she wouldn't get food all over the floor where it doesn't belong."

I have also encountered her sitting beside the litter box, staring into it, waiting for me to notice her and get the message: Aretha will not go in the litter box if there is any residue from previous bathroom activities in there. She assumes I must know this by now, so any infraction of the rules results in a perturbed look and an upturned nose.

10

While it's true that those who are extremely orderly can be a bit rigid, they do help the rest of us rein in our chaotic tendencies. Take a deep breath, remind yourself that they mean well, and be grateful that the food dishes are always in the same place, right where they belong.

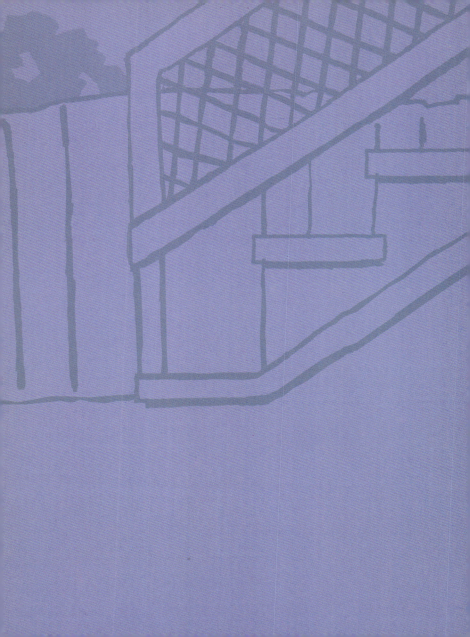

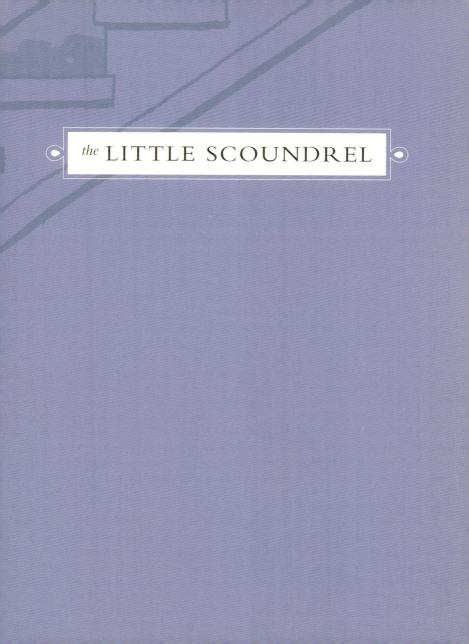

the LITTLE SCOUNDREL

SKEETER'S SUITOR DECIDED to visit again. There he was—skinnier, even more ragged—an intruder trying to come through the cat door. Aretha was napping, so it fell to me to shoo him away—not an easy task. We had an argument on the stairs: I kept telling him to go away, that he couldn't come inside, and he kept meowing angrily and hissing. Then he swatted at my bare feet and scratched me, drawing blood. Uh-oh. What if he's not just a hungry stray, I thought. What if he's mean? I started worrying that Skeeter and Aretha would be attacked in their own home. I envisioned an aggressive cat terrorizing the neighborhood, swiping at the ankles of elderly women and young children. A couple of people I spoke to said I might have to have him euthanized. While I was mad at him, I wasn't that mad.

Instead, I rented a humane trap for the feral little guy, got him at dawn, and took him to my vet's office to have him neutered. Of course, the vet's office wasn't open yet, so we stopped for coffee first. I think it was in the Starbucks parking lot that I began calling him Little Scoundrel. We bonded over early morning coffee. Given that he was about to have his manhood compromised, it was a memorable and meaningful exchange.

The vet told me that he was only about a year old—just a young tyke with a lot of attitude.

At the end of the day, I picked him up—damp from his complimentary flea bath, neutered, still talking up a storm—and we returned to the neighborhood. I had chosen a spot at the end of a quiet cul-de-sac where there is a cluster of trees—part of his familiar turf. A friend met me and we put food and water out for him, then watched as he practically inhaled the food. Then he sauntered off into the trees with a look back at us that seemed to say, "Well, this was quite a day."

I decided to keep putting food and water at that same location every day. I sort of wanted to see the little guy again, but all I found were empty dishes each day—no sign of Scoundrel. All I could do was hope that he was the one getting the food.

LIFE LESSON

11

First impressions are never reliable.
Someone might be having a bad day, or be
ravenously hungry, or frightened. Maybe
all of the above. When someone hisses at
you, consider that they might not really mean
it. Think about giving them another chance,
especially if they are young, small, and talkative. You might just end up liking them.

SCOUNDREL, *the* RETURN

TWO WEEKS AFTER our trip to the vet's office, Scoundrel reappeared outside the door—with a bit more flesh on his bones and a lot less testosterone. Apparently, he had been getting the food I faithfully left for him each day and, even more apparently, had decided he wanted to be part of our little family. He had quickly figured out our schedule, waiting at dawn for the cat door to be opened, and hanging around at the end of the day for me to water the garden so he could follow me around and brush against my legs, meowing constantly.

He was quickly laying claim to my heart, and I convinced myself that we could all be one happy family—three females and a rather talkative male. My two girls didn't see it that way. Skeeter didn't appreciate his rambunctious advances, and Aretha turned into a small Bengal tiger whenever he was near.

But I persisted, certain that it would all work out in time. I put out food and a cat bed for Scoundrel in the garden and visited him every evening as the sun went down, trying to appease my cats as best I could. There were a few times during the day when he came inside and Aretha let him be, filling my heart with hope. But as soon as Scoundrel tried to approach her in the bedroom a terrible fight would ensue.

Things went from bad to worse. Skeeter left for two days. She was nearby—neighbors spotted her, and occasionally I heard her meowing—but she refused to come home. Then Scoundrel and Aretha had a particularly vicious fight before dawn one morning. I knew that was it. I had to find a new home for Scoundrel and restore peace to ours.

After more phone calls than I can count, I called a woman I know in Malibu—one of those rare people who should have honorary wings pinned onto her back by the entire animal kingdom. She will immediately and unhesitatingly help any animal in need. Before ten that morning Scoundrel and I were on our way to Malibu, with me sobbing the entire time. I felt like I had failed him, I was scared he wouldn't find a home, and I was so terribly sad that I had to let him go.

What followed was a reminder that miracles do happen sometimes. Scoundrel was only in my friend's place for an hour after I left. A woman who lived up the hill walked in, saw him, and fell immediately in love. When my phone rang and my friend put

Scoundrel's new mother on the line, I knew I should have had a little more faith that everything would work out fine.

Scoundrel now lives in a lovely house in the Malibu hills with a dog named Rusty and a family who adores him. I have visited him and watched him stroll confidently around the property. His coat is shiny and he is no longer the needy skinny boy he once was. He hunts rodents, studies the horses next door, and lounges in the sun. I've become friends now with his new family, and we all know that this was the home he was always meant to have. He just took a few detours along the way.

12

Not everyone who comes into your life
is supposed to stay there. Sometimes you're
just a way station. Love them while they are
there, love them when they move on, and
trust that we all find our true home eventually.